iOS 17.3 Seniors Guide

A Seniors' Comprehensive Guide to Mastering New Features with Ease and Confidence

Valerie A. Wood

Copyright © [2024] by [Valerie A. Wood]

Table of content

Introduction

In the ever-evolving realm of technology, iOS updates serve as crucial milestones, affecting the digital experiences of millions. iOS 17.3, the latest generation from Apple, not only delivers cutting-edge innovations but also highlights the need to be updated in the digital sphere. This detailed guide will delve into the complicated terrain of iOS 17.3, specifically geared to the needs and interests of elders.

Overview of iOS 17.3

iOS 17.3 is a culmination of Apple's dedication to enhancing the user experience. With a focus on increasing security, introducing unique functionality, and addressing user input, this update stands as a monument to Apple's commitment to creating a seamless and safe digital environment. From incremental enhancements to revolutionary additions, iOS 17.3 is poised to elevate the capabilities of Apple devices.

One major inclusion in iOS 17.3 is the Stolen Device Protection feature. Designed to preserve user data in the unfortunate case of a theft, this security precaution adds an extra degree of protection. Through a precise integration of biometric authentication, such as Face ID and Touch ID, users may strengthen their devices against illegal access. The guide will provide extensive insights into activating and utilizing this function efficiently.

Importance of iOS Updates for Seniors

For seniors, the impact of iOS updates extends beyond the appeal of new features. These updates play a key role in assuring device security, enhancing accessibility, and offering an overall seamless user experience. In a continuously advancing technology landscape, staying current with the newest upgrades becomes synonymous with maintaining a secure and efficient digital lifestyle.

As technology becomes more intertwined with daily activities, the potential risks also increase. iOS releases, including version 17.3, incorporate essential security patches, protecting users from increasing cyber threats. Seniors, often targeted owing to perceived vulnerabilities, will benefit enormously from the additional security features implemented into the current upgrade.

Beyond security, iOS releases routinely add features targeted at boosting accessibility. Larger font and display options, increased voiceover capabilities, and specific magnifier and zoom functions cater to the various demands of elders. This guide will methodically investigate these accessibility options, assuring elders can harness the full power of their Apple gadgets.

Moreover, the progress of iOS underscores Apple's dedication to inclusivity. The inclusion of Collaborative Playlists in Apple Music, a feature making a return in iOS 17.3, illustrates this devotion. Seniors can exploit these collaborative playlists to connect with loved ones through shared musical experiences. The book will explicate the methods for building, editing, and engaging with these playlists seamlessly.

In essence, iOS updates are not just about novelty; they are about empowerment. For seniors, embracing the latest updates equates to access a wealth of features that boost security, foster connectivity, and simplify digital interactions. This tutorial seeks to navigate elders through the rich tapestry of iOS 17.3, helping them to join the digital world with confidence and simplicity.

Chapter I. Getting Started

Updating to iOS 17.3:

Updating your device's operating system is an essential step to guarantee you have access to the latest features, security upgrades, and bug fixes. As of the latest update, iOS 17.3 provides various upgrades, making it necessary for seniors to keep their devices up to date. Here's a thorough guide on how to update to iOS 17.3:

1. Check Device Compatibility:

Before performing the upgrade, confirm that your device is compatible with iOS 17.3. Apple normally offers a list of supported devices for each iOS release. You may get this information on the official Apple website or inside the settings of your device.

2. Connect to a Stable Wi-Fi Network:

To eliminate interruptions during the upgrade process, connect your device to a stable Wi-Fi network. This allows a seamless and effective download of the iOS 17.3 update without relying on cellular data, which could be slower and less dependable.

3. Sufficient Battery Level or Connect to Power:

It's vital to have enough battery power or connect your smartphone to a power source before launching the update. A low battery during the update process could lead to issues or even a stoppage of the installation.

4. Backup Your Data:

Before starting with any big upgrade, it's wise to back up your device. This ensures that your sensitive data, such as images, contacts, and app data, is safe in case something goes wrong during the upgrade. You can use iCloud or iTunes for this reason.

5. Initiate the Update:

Navigate to your device's settings and select "Software Update." If iOS 17.3 is available, you'll see an opportunity to download and install it. Follow the on-screen directions to commence the upgrade process.

6. Wait for the Download and Installation:

The download time varies based on your internet speed and the amount of the update. Once the download is complete, your device will immediately begin the installation procedure. This can take some time, so be patient and avoid disturbing the process.

7. Complete the Setup:

After the installation is complete, your device will restart, and you'll be prompted to complete the setup. This may entail entering your Apple ID password, confirming preferences, and agreeing to new terms and conditions.

Navigating the Home Screen:

The home screen is the center hub of your iOS device, acting as the starting point for accessing apps, functions, and settings. Navigating the home screen efficiently is crucial to a seamless user experience. Here's a complete guide on how elders can use the home screen properly on iOS 17.3:

1. Understanding App Icons:

Each app on your home screen is represented by an icon. These icons are meant for rapid recognition, and their placement can be adjusted. Tap on an icon to open the related app.

2. Organizing Apps:

Long-press on any app icon until it enters jiggle mode. In this mode, you can rearrange app icons by dragging them to new places. You can also create folders by dragging one app icon onto another, helping to organize your home screen.

3. Using the Dock:

The dock, placed at the bottom of the screen, allows you to access frequently used apps from any home screen page. You can customize the dock by placing your most-used apps for quick and simple access.

4. Swipe Gestures:

Swiping left or right on the home screen allows you to navigate between different pages of apps. This is particularly useful if you have multiple apps and wish to organize them into separate pages.

5. Search for Apps:

If you have multiple apps and find it tough to discover a certain one, use the search tool. Swipe down on the home screen, and a search bar will emerge. Type the name of the app, and iOS will recommend suitable results.

6. Accessing Widgets:

iOS 17 featured widgets that deliver at-a-glance information from apps on your home screen. Swipe to the right on the home screen to reach the widget panel. Customize widgets based on your choices and needs.

Understanding Icons and Buttons:

Icons and buttons are graphic elements that facilitate interaction with your device. iOS 17.3 maintains a user-friendly interface with intuitive icons and controls. Here's an in-depth analysis of common icons and buttons elders may encounter:

1. Home Button:

In prior iOS versions, the home button was a physical button situated in the bottom center of the device. However, with subsequent iPhone models, the home button is replaced by swiping motions. To get back to the home screen, swipe upward from the bottom.

2. App Icons:

App icons are graphical representations of applications installed on your smartphone. Each icon is designed to be recognized and indicative of the app's usefulness. Tap an app icon to launch the related application.

3. Settings Icon:

The Settings app, symbolized by a gear icon, is where you may configure many aspects of your smartphone. It's a key tool for modifying preferences, managing accounts, and configuring security settings.

4. Notification Center:

To view the Notification Center, swipe down from the top of the screen. Here, you'll find notifications from apps, calendar events, and other pertinent information. Clear notifications by swiping them away.

5. Control Center:

Access the Control Center by swiping down from the top-right corner (or swiping up from the bottom on previous versions). Here, you may toggle settings such as Wi-Fi, Bluetooth, and screen brightness.

6. Battery Icon:

The battery icon, normally situated in the top-right corner, represents your device's current battery level. Charging status is also displayed, and touching the icon provides more specific information on battery usage.

7. App Switcher:

On devices without a physical home button, swipe up from the bottom and hold to open the app switcher. Here, you can see and switch between previously used apps.

8. Volume and Silent Mode:

Physical buttons on the side of your device control volume. Additionally, there's a switch for toggling between silent and ringing modes.

Understanding these important characteristics of iOS 17.3 ensures that seniors can confidently use their devices, access essential functions, and fully enjoy the benefits of the latest software upgrade.

Chapter II. Stolen Device Protection

Enabling Stolen Device Protection on iOS 17.3 is a key step towards safeguarding your iPhone and the sensitive information it stores. In this detailed guide, we'll go into the process of enabling this security feature, investigate the integration of Face ID and Touch ID for increased safety, and explain how managing sensitive settings with a security delay can fortify the defensive mechanisms against potential threats.

Enabling Stolen Device Protection

Stolen Device Protection is a new and significant feature added in iOS 17.3, aimed to give an additional degree of security in case your iPhone slips into the wrong hands. To enable this functionality, perform these simple steps:

1. Update to iOS 17.3:

Ensure your smartphone is running the newest iOS version. Go to Settings > General > Software Update and download/install iOS 17.3 if you haven't already.

2. Access Stolen Device Protection:

Navigate to Settings on your iPhone and pick Face ID and Passcode. Here, you will discover the option for Stolen Device Protection.

3. Enable Stolen Device Protection:

Toggle the switch to enable Stolen Device Protection. You might be prompted to authenticate using Face ID or Touch ID, adding an added degree of protection to the activation process.

4. Biometric Authentication Setup:

Stolen Device Protection involves biometric authentication, leveraging technologies like Face ID and Touch ID. Ensure your device has these functionalities set up and configured appropriately.

5. Security Prompts:

Once active, you may notice security alerts when accessing some sensitive settings or information on your device. These prompts are deliberate and serve as a barrier against unauthorized access.

6. Testing the Feature:

Perform a few test scenarios to familiarize yourself with how Stolen Device Protection works. Attempt to access important settings, and see the additional security mechanisms in effect.

Using Face ID and Touch ID for Security

The integration of Face ID and Touch ID in iOS 17.3 extends beyond unlocking your device; it plays a critical role in increasing the security of Stolen Device Protection. Here's how you can employ these biometric authentication methods effectively:

1. Biometric Setup:

Ensure Face ID or Touch ID is set up on your smartphone. You may find these choices in the Face ID and Passcode settings.

2.Biometric Authentication for Sensitive Actions:

With Stolen Device Protection enabled, biometric verification becomes a necessity for accessing saved passwords, changing essential settings, or performing activities that contain sensitive information.

3. Security Delay for Added Protection:

Face ID and Touch ID not only function as gatekeepers but also introduce a security delay for certain actions. This delay is an intentional mechanism to avoid fast and unauthorized alterations.

4. Recognizing Familiar Locations:

iOS 17.3 is meant to recognize familiar settings, such as your home or business, eliminating the need for security delays in these trusted environments.

Managing Sensitive Settings with Security Delay

One of the important features of Stolen Device Protection is the introduction of a security delay for particular actions. This delay functions as a buffer, needing additional time before essential settings, like Apple ID password changes, may be adjusted. Here's a detailed look at managing sensitive settings:

1. Understanding Security Delay:

When attempting to make changes to critical settings, iOS 17.3 introduces a security delay. This delay assures that even if an unauthorized user gains access to your device, they won't be able to make significant modifications rapidly.

2. Face ID and Touch ID Integration:

Biometric authentication is linked with the security delay, guaranteeing that only authorized users can expedite the process by authenticating with Face ID or Touch ID.

3. No Delay in Trusted Locations:

The security delay is intelligent, exempting trustworthy places from the delay requirement. This means that while you're at familiar places like work or home, you can make changes without the additional wait.

4. Customizing Delay choices:

iOS 17.3 allows users to adjust security delay choices to a certain extent. Explore the settings to alter delays based on your preferences and usage habits.

iOS 17.3's Stolen Device Protection, paired with Face ID and Touch ID integration, marks a huge leap in securing your iPhone and its data. By enabling these features and understanding how to manage sensitive settings properly, you empower your device with comprehensive defenses against potential threats. Stay watchful, maintain your biometric authentication methods up to date, and investigate the customization options available to personalize the security features to your needs.

Chapter III. Apple Music Collaborative Playlists: Enhancing Your Musical Experience Together

Music has long been a worldwide language, bringing people together through common melodies and rhythms. With iOS 17.3, Apple provides an exciting tool to amplify this connection — Collaborative Playlists in Apple Music. In this detailed guide, we'll go into the introduction, creation, editing, and interaction components of Collaborative Playlists, equipping you with the information to make your musical journey more collaborative and pleasurable.

Introduction to Collaborative Playlists

Collaborative Playlists transform the way you enjoy music, allowing you to construct and share playlists seamlessly with friends, family, or anyone who shares your musical taste. Imagine making a playlist for a road trip together or agreeing on the right soundtrack for a gathering — Collaborative Playlists make these situations a reality.

To get started, open Apple Music and browse the "Playlists" section. Here, you'll find the opportunity to create a new playlist. With Collaborative Playlists, you can now ask others to contribute, turning music selection into a collaborative experience.

Explore the social component of music by discovering how Collaborative Playlists build a sense of community through shared musical performances. Discover the delight of co-creating playlists that resonate with the collective soul of your group.

Creating and Editing Shared Playlists

Creating a Collaborative Playlist is an easy process that begins with selecting "New Playlist" and toggling the "Collaborative" switch. Once active, you may invite others to join your playlist by sharing an invitation link or directly through their Apple Music profiles.

Dive into the complexities of playlist construction by examining the different customization choices. Add an intriguing title and description to give your playlist identity. Learn how to arrange and organize your recordings for a seamless listening experience.

Editing a Collaborative Playlist is a collaborative undertaking, with contributors having the power to add, remove, or rearrange music. Uncover the collaborative potential by knowing the etiquette of playlist editing – respecting each other's musical preferences while contributing to a harmonic blend of sounds.

Interacting with Collaborative Playlists

Interacting with Collaborative Playlists goes beyond the creation phase. Discover how to explore and join existing Collaborative Playlists that correspond with your musical likes. Navigate through the Apple Music community to uncover playlists created by friends, influencers, or fellow music aficionados.

Explore the unique elements that enhance your interaction with Collaborative Playlists. From writing comments on specific songs to reacting with emojis, grasp the different ways you can share your views and gratitude inside the Apple Music ecosystem.

Uncover the possibility of discovering new music through collaboration. With numerous contributions, Collaborative Playlists become dynamic, reflecting varied preferences and introducing you to songs you might have ignored. Learn how to use this joint effort for a deeper and more expansive musical trip.

Collaborative Playlists in Apple Music herald a new era of shared musical experiences. This feature not only transforms the way we curate playlists but also fosters a sense of community and connection through the universal language of music. Embrace the collaborative spirit, build unique playlists together, and let the harmonious notes of shared songs resound within your social circles. iOS 17.3 draws people together through the power of music, making every playlist a collaborative masterpiece.

Chapter IV. Accessibility Features for Seniors in iOS

As technology improves, ensuring accessibility becomes a key priority, especially for seniors who may experience difficulty in accessing small print and sophisticated interfaces. iOS 17.3 introduces a series of accessibility features meant to make the iPhone experience more inclusive for elders. Let's go into these features and discover how they can greatly boost user experience.

Larger Text and Display Options

One of the noteworthy features for seniors in iOS 17.3 is the ability to modify text size and display settings for greater visibility. Navigating through menus, reading messages, and engaging with programs become more comfortable with larger font. To enable this function, users can visit to Settings > Display & Brightness > Text Size. Here, a simple slider allows for easy modification of font size according to individual preferences.

Moreover, iOS 17.3 includes extra display settings that cater to seniors' various needs. The option to change contrast, raise bold lettering, and adjust color filters can dramatically enhance the clarity of on-screen content. Exploring these choices within Settings > Accessibility > Display & Text Size offers a world of personalization, empowering seniors to personalize their iPhone display to match their requirements.

VoiceOver for Audio Feedback

VoiceOver, a pioneering feature on iOS devices, is an important component of accessibility for seniors. In iOS 17.3, VoiceOver continues to deliver auditory feedback, detailing on-screen components and actions. For seniors with visual impairments, VoiceOver becomes an invaluable tool, delivering a spoken description of the selected item and guiding them through the interface.

Enabling VoiceOver is straightforward. Users can access Settings > Accessibility > VoiceOver to activate this function. Once enabled, seniors can explore various movements to navigate around apps, read text, and interact with things on the screen. iOS 17.3's VoiceOver upgrades offer a more smooth and intuitive experience, making the iPhone a more accessible device for seniors with visual impairments.

Magnifier and Zoom Features

Magnifier and Zoom capabilities significantly boost the accessibility toolset for elders in iOS 17.3. These functionalities are aimed to aid those with low vision by providing ways to magnify and zoom into on-screen content.

The Magnifier feature transforms the iPhone camera into a magnifying glass, allowing seniors to zoom in on printed material, small objects, or anything requiring a closer look. To enable the Magnifier, users can triple-press the side or home button and access it through Settings > Accessibility > Magnifier.

The Zoom function, on the other hand, offers a system-wide magnification option. By heading to Settings > Accessibility > Zoom, seniors can enable this option and choose the level of magnification. Once triggered, a simple double-tap with three fingers allows users to zoom in and out, making it easier to read text, view photographs, or traverse sophisticated interfaces.

Also, iOS 17.3's accessibility features for seniors constitute a remarkable effort by Apple to build a more inclusive digital world. The larger font and display settings, together with VoiceOver, Magnifier, and Zoom capabilities, cater to the different needs of seniors, giving them the tools to manage and use their iPhones with more ease. As technology continues to progress, the dedication to accessibility guarantees that seniors can confidently embrace the benefits of their iOS devices, enabling independence and involvement in the digital era.

Chapter V. Understanding StandBy Mode

StandBy Mode in iOS 17.3 is a dynamic feature designed to transform your iPhone into a smart display when charging horizontally. This immersive experience presents critical information such as the time, calendar events, photographs, and notifications in easily accessible, big blocks. For elders, this mode offers a comfortable approach to assimilating information with just a glance.

StandBy Mode functions as a digital dashboard, enabling quick access to vital data without requiring substantial input.

When enabled, it converts the charging iPhone into a visual hub, delivering a snapshot of pertinent information. This introduction lays the framework for investigating the customization options and notification management under StandBy Mode.

Customizing StandBy Settings

To really adapt StandBy Mode to individual preferences, iOS 17.3 gives a range of customization choices. Seniors can navigate to the Settings menu, discover the StandBy area, and delve into a range of settings to personalize their experience.

Within the customization options, users can alter the types of information presented during StandBy, picking from selections including time, calendar events, and images. This feature ensures that seniors may prioritize what matters most to them, optimizing the visual design to boost usability.

Furthermore, font size and color options are accessible to people with special visual preferences. The option to alter these settings fits various needs, allowing seniors to optimize their StandBy experience for readability and comfort.

Managing Notifications in StandBy

While StandBy Mode provides a simple overview of essential information, controlling alerts within this mode adds an extra layer of control. Seniors can decide which notifications are visible during StandBy, ensuring that the experience remains focused on vital developments.

In the StandBy settings, users can change the "Show Notifications" option on or off. This basic yet useful control affects whether notifications are displayed on the StandBy screen. For people who value privacy or desire to limit distractions, removing this option offers a more discreet StandBy experience.

However, iOS 17.3 acknowledges the necessity of crucial notifications, like weather situations. To solve this, a modified method allows vital warnings to still be presented in StandBy mode even when general notifications are turned off. This balance ensures that seniors remain informed about important concerns while having control over less pressing information.

For extra granularity in handling alerts, users can investigate the "Show Preview on Top Only" feature. Enabling this option guarantees that only a summary preview of notifications is revealed, retaining a sense of privacy while yet providing a look at incoming messages or alerts.

iOS 17.3's StandBy Mode is a versatile tool that caters to the special demands of seniors. By grasping the subtleties of this feature, changing its settings, and handling notifications properly, seniors may harness the power of their iPhones in a way that corresponds with their tastes and enhances their overall user experience.

Chapter VI. Siri Enhancements: Unlocking the Power of Voice Control in iOS 17.3

In the ever-evolving universe of iOS releases, Siri remains a loyal partner for customers seeking hands-free interactions with their smartphones. With the release of iOS 17.3, Siri experiences substantial enhancements, making it even more intuitive and responsive. In this research, we delve into the complexities of these upgrades, from the iconic "Hey Siri" activation to fine-tuning sensitivity and utilizing the potential of voice commands.

Activating Siri with "Hey Siri"

A cornerstone of Siri's functioning, the "Hey Siri" activation phrase exemplifies convenience. In iOS 17.3, this function undergoes modifications aiming at smooth involvement. Users may now effortlessly awaken Siri just by uttering the famous phrase, removing the need for extra prompts. This feature streamlines accessibility, particularly for elders who may find a simplified trigger advantageous.

The "Hey Siri" capability extends beyond basic activation. With iOS 17.3, Siri demonstrates heightened responsiveness, ensuring a rapid and accurate acknowledgment of user orders. This development is a testament to Apple's commitment to optimizing the user experience and understanding the essential role Siri plays in daily device interactions.

Adjusting Siri's Sensitivity

Recognizing the broad user population, iOS 17.3 delivers an unparalleled level of customization with regard to Siri's sensitivity. Users may now tune Siri's responsiveness to their preferences, creating a harmonious balance between a sharp ear for orders and a polite awareness of ambient noise.

Navigating via the levels menu, users will discover the ability to fine-tune Siri's sensitivity levels. Whether in a crowded city or a peaceful house, this function guarantees that Siri adapts to the user's environment, boosting the overall reliability of voice interactions. For seniors, who may prefer a tailored and adaptive Siri experience, this personalization option gives a newfound sense of power.

Utilizing Voice Commands

Voice commands sit at the foundation of Siri's utility, translating verbal instructions into practical responses. iOS 17.3 extends this feature, boosting Siri's repertory of commands and strengthening its grasp of natural language. Users may now issue a broader spectrum of requests, ranging from setting reminders and sending messages to managing smart home devices with unsurpassed precision.

Seniors, typically drawn to voice-controlled features for their simplicity, will find iOS 17.3's increased voice command functionality particularly empowering. Siri becomes a trusted aide, capable of accomplishing tasks with a nuanced comprehension of verbal cues. This evolution reflects Apple's dedication to making voice commands a versatile and vital component of the iOS experience.

Beyond the Surface: Practical Applications for Seniors

The influence of these Siri advancements reaches far beyond the surface, influencing how seniors interact with their devices on a regular basis. "Hey, Siri" becomes a verbal doorway to a myriad of functions, allowing seniors to effortlessly check the weather, send emotional notes, or conduct a hands-free chat with a loved one.

Customizing Siri's sensitivity gives seniors a bespoke experience, responding to individual preferences and comfort levels. Whether customers prefer a more responsive Siri in a quiet situation or a less obtrusive contact in a bustling one, the freedom to modify sensitivity ensures that Siri adjusts to their particular demands.

The enlarged vocabulary of voice commands not only streamlines chores but also fosters a more natural and conversational engagement with technology. Seniors may dictate messages, ask for directions, or even operate smart home gadgets via intuitive voice prompts. This seamless incorporation of voice commands into daily activities promotes accessibility for seniors, eliminating reliance on manual interactions and potentially minimizing any issues associated with traditional touch-based navigation.

Looking Ahead: Siri's Role in Future iOS Developments

As iOS continues to improve, Siri's function as a virtual assistant is ready to evolve further. The advancements offered in iOS 17.3 serve as a testament to Apple's commitment to perfecting the user experience, particularly for seniors who may benefit from an intuitive and voice-centric approach to device interaction.

The trip through Siri's advancements in iOS 17.3 shows a landscape where technology becomes a seamless extension of the user's intent. "Hey Siri," once a trigger, now becomes a customized invitation to a world of possibilities, where voice instructions are not merely recognized but anticipated. Adjusting sensitivity emerges as a subtle yet meaningful tweak, emphasizing the idea that technology should adapt to the user, not the other way around.

iOS 17.3 elevates Siri from a mere virtual assistant to a personalized and responsive partner. Seniors, in particular, stand to gain enormous value from these advancements, as Siri gets more sensitive to their tastes and smoothly fits into their everyday lives. As we embrace the future of iOS, Siri remains a beacon of innovation, demonstrating that the power of voice extends far beyond just words – it's a bridge to a more accessible and user-centric digital universe.

Chapter VII. Exploring Additional Tips for Seniors on iOS 17.3

As technology continues to progress, it's crucial for seniors to feel comfortable utilizing the latest capabilities on their iPhones. iOS 17.3 provides several changes, and in this chapter, we will look into three more suggestions suited to seniors: utilizing the Live Voicemail feature, setting up Contact Posters, and discovering the hidden gems within iOS 17.

Using Live Voicemail Feature

The Live Voicemail feature in iOS 17.3 gives a new way for seniors to interact with their voicemail messages. Unlike standard voicemail systems, Live Voicemail allows customers to listen to voicemails as they are being recorded in real-time. This not only increases the entire voicemail experience but also offers seniors greater control and convenience.

To access Live Voicemail, open the Phone app and select the Voicemail tab. When a voicemail is received, instead of playing it again after it's entirely recorded, users can select to listen in real-time. This feature is particularly advantageous for people who want a more immediate and involved approach to handling their voicemails.

Seniors can also take advantage of extra choices inside Live Voicemail, such as pausing, rewinding, or fast-forwarding during replay. This permits individuals to navigate through texts with ease, ensuring they catch every vital aspect without any difficulty.

Setting Up Contact Posters

Contact Posters are a unique and personalized way to enhance the calling experience on iOS 17.3. This tool allows seniors to link certain visuals with their contacts, making it easier to identify incoming calls and creating a more visually engaging communication experience.

To set up Contact Posters, click on the Contacts app and select the contact you wish to modify. Choose the "Edit" option and look for the option to add a photo. Seniors can either shoot a new photo using their device's camera or select an existing photo from their gallery. This visual representation of contacts adds a personal touch to the calling experience, making it more fun and memorable.

Additionally, Contact Posters can be very effective for the elderly who may have vision or cognitive difficulties. Associating faces with names adds an additional layer of identification and can help to a more inclusive and accessible smartphone experience.

Exploring Hidden iOS 17 Features

iOS 17.3 comes with a variety of capabilities, and some hidden gems may go undetected without a bit of study. Seniors can benefit immensely from unearthing these hidden features, as they often bring new functionality and shortcuts that enhance the overall user experience.

One such hidden feature is the option to modify the Control Center. By heading to

Settings > Control Center, seniors can add or remove numerous shortcuts and widgets according to their preferences. This customization guarantees that the Control Center is personalized to their unique needs, allowing rapid access to commonly used functions.

Another hidden gem is the upgraded Autocorrect feature. Seniors can fine-tune Autocorrect settings by navigating to Settings > General > Keyboard. Adjusting options like autocorrection sensitivity and adding personalized shortcuts can dramatically improve the typing experience, responding to individual preferences and habits.

iOS 17.3 delivers not just apparent enhancements but also a range of functions that can considerably improve the smartphone experience for seniors. By adopting Live Voicemail, setting up Contact Posters, and investigating secret iOS 17 features, seniors may unleash a world of possibilities and make the most out of their iPhones. These ideas seek to empower elders, ensuring they feel confident and proficient in utilizing the latest improvements in smartphone technology.

Chapter VIII. Troubleshooting and Support

In the dynamic world of technology, even the most advanced systems can experience challenges. iOS 17.3, while laden with features tailored to elders, is no exception. This section will look into typical challenges users could experience and present practical solutions. Additionally, we will cover the numerous channels where elders might seek assistance when experiencing issues beyond the scope of self-resolution.

Common Issues and Solutions

1. Device Performance Slowdowns:
Seniors may notice a decline in their device's performance after updating to iOS 17.3. This could be attributable to background processes or incompatible programs. To address this, users can:
- Close superfluous apps running in the background.
- Check for app updates in the App Store.
- Restart the device to refresh system resources.

2. Stolen Device Protection Activation:
Enabling Stolen Device Protection is an essential security protection, however, users could encounter issues throughout the activation procedure. To troubleshoot:
- Ensure that Face ID and Touch ID are correctly set up.

- Verify that biometric authentication is being used as required.
- Contact Apple Support for tailored assistance if troubles persist.

3. Collaborative Playlists Not Syncing:

Some seniors could have issues with collaborative playlists not syncing between devices. To resolve this:

- Check the internet connection on the device.
- Ensure that Apple Music settings allow for collaborative playlist sharing.
- Verify that all participants are on iOS 17.3 or newer.

4. Accessibility Features Adjustment:

Tailoring accessibility features to individual preferences is key. If adjustments are not working as expected:

- Review the settings for larger text, display options, and voice commands.
- Restart the device after making modifications.

- Seek assistance from a tech-savvy friend or family member.

5. StandBy Mode Display Issues:

Users encountering troubles with StandBy Mode's display might perform the following steps:

- Adjust settings under the StandBy Mode section.
- Toggle off and on the StandBy Mode feature.
- If troubles persist, consider contacting Apple Support.

Where to Seek Help

1.Apple Support Website:

The official Apple Support website is a helpful resource for elders facing issues. It includes a rich knowledge base with step-by-step guides and troubleshooting articles. Users can visit support.apple.com and search for specific issues to find pertinent information.

2. Apple Support App:

The Apple Support app, available on the App Store, provides a user-friendly interface for requesting support. Seniors can use the app to chat with Apple Support, arrange phone conversations, or even set up appointments at Apple Stores for in-person help.

3. Community Forums:

Engaging with the Apple community can be useful. Platforms like the Apple Support Communities allow consumers to post questions, exchange experiences, and receive insights from other users and Apple aficionados. Seniors can find solace in knowing that they are not alone in their problems.

4. Local Apple Store:

For seniors who prefer face-to-face support, visiting a local Apple Store can be a wonderful choice. Apple's store personnel is trained to assist people with numerous concerns, from hardware faults to software troubleshooting.

5. Tech-Savvy Family and Friends:

Sometimes, a helping hand from a tech-savvy family member or friend can make a major difference. Seniors can call out to loved ones for support, especially if they want individual aid in navigating iOS 17.3.

In conclusion, troubleshooting and seeking support are vital components of adapting to new technologies. iOS 17.3, created with elders in mind, offers a plethora of capabilities, and with the appropriate direction, any obstacles faced can be overcome. Whether through self-help methods, online resources, or in-person support, seniors may embrace the full potential of their iOS devices and stay engaged in the ever-evolving digital ecosystem.

Conclusion

In the ever-evolving field of technology, iOS 17.3 provides a plethora of features aimed at better the user experience, and seniors are no exception to this technological growth. As we complete this tour, let's go into a comprehensive overview of the important features examined and present an encouraging perspective for seniors to embrace and explore the capabilities of iOS 17.3.

Recap of Key Features

1. Stolen Device Protection:
- iOS 17.3 introduces a vital security update with Stolen Device Protection.
- Enabling this option adds an extra degree of security in case of device

theft, requiring biometric identification for sensitive actions.
- Face ID and Touch ID play essential roles in safeguarding the user's data and sensitive settings.

2. Apple Music Collaborative Playlists:
- The return of collaborative playlists in Apple Music offers a social dimension to music sharing.
- Seniors can create, update, and participate in shared playlists, promoting a sense of connection through shared musical experiences.

3. Accessibility Features:
- iOS 17.3 stresses inclusivity with expanded accessibility features.
- Larger text and display options cater to seniors with visual impairments, ensuring a comfortable and personalized viewing experience.

- VoiceOver delivers audio feedback, making navigation seamless and intuitive.
- Magnifier and zoom functions permit users to tailor their device according to individual needs.

4. StandBy Mode:
- Understanding and modifying StandBy Mode allows seniors to make their iPhones into smart screens while charging horizontally.
- Managing notifications in StandBy ensures a balance between remaining informed and maintaining privacy.

5. Siri Enhancements:
- Activating Siri with a simple "Hey Siri" or altering sensitivity caters to varied user preferences.
- Utilizing voice commands simplifies engagement with the gadget, making it a helpful tool for seniors wanting hands-free functioning.

6. Additional Tips for Seniors:

- Exploring the Live Voicemail feature and creating Contact Posters provides a personal touch to communication.
- Unveiling secret iOS 17 features gives up options for customization and discovering functionalities that may enhance the overall user experience.

Encouragement for Seniors to Explore iOS 17.3

As technology improves, it is reasonable that adopting new features could appear daunting, especially for seniors who may not have grown up in the digital age. However, iOS 17.3 is not simply an update; it's an opportunity for seniors to expand their digital lives, staying connected, entertained, and informed.

Embracing Change:

Change can be daunting, but it also presents chances for growth. Embracing the new capabilities in iOS 17.3 can open doors to a more personalized and engaging user experience.

Personalized Learning:

Apple develops its applications with user-friendliness in mind. Seniors can take advantage of resources like this guide, Apple's support material, and community forums to personalize their learning journey.

Tech at Your Own Pace:

There's no rush to embrace every feature immediately. Seniors can experience iOS 17.3 at their own speed, focusing on one feature at a time and gradually incorporating them into their regular routine.

Stay Connected:

The linked world we live in today stresses the need to remain connected. iOS 17.3 enhances this connectivity, letting seniors exchange music, communicate effortlessly, and participate with their digital devices in meaningful ways.

Tech Support and Assistance:
 For those moments of uncertainty or when seeking further guidance, tech support and community aid are readily available. Apple's support channels and community forums give a plethora of information and assistance dedicated to seniors.

In conclusion, iOS 17.3 is not just a software update; it's a gateway to a more enriching and tailored digital experience for seniors. By knowing and embracing the essential elements highlighted in this guide, seniors may traverse the digital landscape with confidence, staying connected, informed, and entertained. As technology continues to improve, so does the possibility for seniors to have full and connected lives in the digital era.